PUBLIC LIBRARY
DISTRICT OF COLUMBIA

HERE WE COME A' PIPING
Book II

HERE WE COME A' PIPING

Chosen by ROSE FYLEMAN

BOOK II

BASIL BLACKWELL · OXFORD

First published August, 1936
Reprinted . . June, 1937
Reprinted December, 1938
Reprinted . . April, 1943
Reprinted . January, 1948

Printed in Great Britain by
Billing and Sons Ltd., Guildford and Esher

ACKNOWLEDGMENTS

The Editor and Publisher gratefully acknowledge permission to reprint the following copyright Poems:

'My Lady,' by Mrs Joan Coster.

'The Lost Shoe,' by Mr Walter de la Mare, by kind consent of Messrs J. B. Pinker & Son.

'Light the Lamps up Lamplighter,' by Miss Eleanor Farjeon.

'Song in Spring,' from A POMANDER OF VERSE, by E. Nesbit, by permission of Messrs John Lane, the Bodley Head.

ACKNOWLEDGMENTS

'A Song for Hal,' by Mrs Laura Richards.

'Hurt no Living Thing,' 'When Cows Come Home,' 'Caterpillar' and 'City Mouse and Garden Mouse,' by permission of Messrs Macmillan & Co., Ltd. taken from THE POETICAL WORKS OF CHRISTINA ROSSETTI.

'From a Railway Carriage,' by Robert Louis Stevenson, reprinted by permission of Mr Lloyd Osbourne.

'Of Myself and My Bath,' by Wilfrid Thorley, from CLOUD-CUCKOOLAND, published by Messrs Macmillan & Co., Ltd.

'Cuckoo,' by Katherine Tynan, reprinted by permission of Miss Pamela Hinkson.

'Kings Came Riding,' by Charles Williams, by permission of the Oxford University Press.

CONTENTS

HURT NO LIVING THING

Hurt no Living Thing	*Christina Rossetti*	2
To the Lady-Bird	*Charlotte T. Smith*	3
Little Trotty Wagtail	*John Clare*	4
Cuckoo	*Katherine Tynan*	6
The Little Fish that Would Not Do as it Was Bid	*Ann & Jane Taylor*	8
When the Cows Come Home	*Christina Rossetti*	10
The Worm	*E. Turner*	11
Cats	*E. C. Brereton*	12
The Boy and the Sheep	*Ann Taylor*	13
The Woodmouse	*Mary Howitt*	15
Caterpillar	*Christina Rossetti*	16
When Jenny Wren was Young		17

PATHWAYS EVERYWHERE

Dust	*M. Isabel Foster*	20
The Tide	*Marjorie Wilson*	21
I've Been Roaming	*George Darley*	22
If Only...	*Rose Fyleman*	23
From a Railway Carriage	*R. L. Stevenson*	25
The Lost Doll	*Charles Kingsley*	26
About Birds-Nesting	*Old Rhyme*	27
Weather Wisdom		28
Secrets	*Luisa Hewitt*	29
My Lady	*Joan Coster*	30
In May		31
Song in Spring	*E. Nesbit*	32

City Mouse and Garden Mouse	*Christina Rossetti*	33
Mousikie		34
Maria's Purse	*Elizabeth Turner*	35
Of Myself and My Bath	*Wilfrid Thorley*	36
Love Between Brothers and Sisters	*Isaac Watts*	37
A Child's Grace	*Robert Burns*	38
Good night	*Jane Taylor*	39
Hush-a-Ba, Birdie		40

WELL I NEVER

Every One	*A. Thatcher*	42
Gossip	*Rose Fyleman*	43
The Four Presents		45
A Spanish Rhyme	*Translated by Rose Fyleman*	47
The Lobster Quadrille	*Lewis Carroll*	48
The Three Welshmen		50
Tom Thimble	*Blanche Winder*	53
Jonathan	*Translated by Rose Fyleman*	55
The Lost Shoe	*Walter de la Mare*	56
A Song for Hal	*Laura Richards*	59
The Frog and the Crow		63

DREAMS AND STARSHINE

The Little Dreamer	*D'A. W. Thompson*	68
Light the Lamps up Lamplighter	*Eleanor Farjeon*	69
Kings Came Riding	*Charles Williams*	72
Cradle Hymn	*Translated from Martin Luther*	74
Old Carol		75

HURT NO LIVING THING

Hurt no living thing;
Ladybird, nor butterfly,
Nor moth with dusty wing,
Nor cricket chirping cheerily,
Nor grasshopper so light of leap,
Nor dancing gnat, nor beetle fat,
Nor harmless worms that creep.

Christina Rossetti

TO THE LADY-BIRD

Lady-bird! Lady-bird! fly away home,
  The field-mouse is gone to her nest;
The daisies have shut up their sleepy red eyes,
  And the birds and the bees are at rest.

Lady-bird! Lady-bird! fly away home;
  The glow-worm is lighting her lamp,
The dew's falling fast, and your fine speck-
    led wings
  Will be wet with the close-clinging damp.

Lady-bird! Lady-bird! fly away home;
  The fairy bells tinkle afar;
Make haste, or they'll catch you and harness
    you fast
  With a cobweb to Oberon's car!

Charlotte T. Smith

LITTLE TROTTY WAGTAIL

LITTLE Trotty Wagtail,
   he went in the rain,
And twittering, tottering sideways,
   he ne'er got straight again;
He stopped to get a worm,
   and looked up to get a fly,
And then he flew away
   ere his feathers they were dry.

Little Trotty Wagtail

Little Trotty Wagtail,
    he waddled in the mud,
And left his little footmarks,
    trample where he would.
He waddled in the water-pudge,
    and waggle went his tail,
And chirrupt up his wings to dry
    upon the garden rail.

Little Trotty Wagtail,
    you nimble all about,
And in the dimpling water-pudge
    you waddle in and out;
Your home is nigh at hand,
    and in the warm pigsty,
So, little Master Wagtail,
    I'll bid you a good-bye.

                      John Clare

CUCKOO

His voice runs before me; I follow; it flies;
It is now in the meadow and now in the skies;
So blithesome, so lightsome; now distant, now here;
And when he calls 'Cuckoo!' the summer is near.

At the first blast of winter, so sad and forespent,
He calls back the roses, red roses, that went
With the dew in their bosoms, young roses and dear,
And when he calls 'Cuckoo!' the summer is near.

Cuckoo

I would twine him a gold cage, but what
 would he do
For his world of the emerald, his bath in the
 blue?
And his wee feathered comrades to make
 him good cheer?
And when he calls 'Cuckoo!' the summer is
 near.

Now, blackbird, give over your harping of
 gold!
Brown thrush and green linnet, your music
 withold!
The flutes of the forest are silver and clear,
But when he calls 'Cuckoo!' the summer is
 near.

Katherine Tynan

THE LITTLE FISH THAT WOULD NOT DO AS IT WAS BID

'Dear mother,' said a little fish,
'Pray is not that a fly?
I'm very hungry, and I wish
You'd let me go and try.'

'Sweet innocent,' the mother cried,
And started from her nook,
'That horrid fly is put to hide
The sharpness of the hook.'

Now, as I've heard, this little trout
Was young and foolish too,
And so he thought he'd venture out,
To see if it were true.

The Little Fish

And round about the hook he played,
With many a longing look,
And—'Dear me,' to himself he said,
'I'm sure that's not a hook.

'I can but give one little pluck:
Let's see, and so I will.'
So on he went, and lo! it stuck
Quite through his little gill.

And as he faint and fainter grew,
With hollow voice he cried,
'Dear mother, had I minded you,
I need not now have died.'

Ann and Jane Taylor

WHEN THE COWS COME HOME

WHEN the cows come home the milk is coming,
Honey's made while the bees are humming;
Duck and drake on the rushy lake,
And the deer live safe in the breezy brake;
And timid, funny, brisk little bunny
Winks his nose and sits all sunny.

                                      Christina Rossetti

THE WORM

As Sally sat upon the ground,
A little crawling worm she found
    Among the garden dirt;
And when she saw the worm she scream'd,
And ran away and cried, and seem'd
    As if she had been hurt.

Mamma, afraid some serious harm
Made Sally scream, was in alarm,
    And left the parlour then;
But when the cause she came to learn,
She bade her daughter back return
    To see the worm again.

The worm they found kept writhing round
Until it sank beneath the ground;
    And Sally learned that day,
That worms are very harmless things,
With neither teeth, nor claws, nor stings
    To frighten her away.

E. Turner

CATS

WHEN the wind is in the east
    The cat is but a lazy beast,
She sits beside the fire and wishes
For nice hot bits from nice hot dishes.

But when the wind is in the west
The cat slips out demurely dressed,
And sidles up the sunny street,
With velvet slippers on her feet.

                          E. C. Brereton

THE BOY AND THE SHEEP

'LAZY sheep, pray tell me why
In the pleasant field you lie,
Eating grass and daisies white,
From the morning till the night:
Everything can something do;
But what kind of use are you?'

'Nay, my little master, nay,
Do not serve me so, I pray!
Don't you see the wool that grows
On my back to make your clothes?
Cold, ah, very cold you'd be
If you had not wool from me.

'True, it seems a pleasant thing
Nipping daisies in the spring;
But what chilly nights I pass
On the cold and dewy grass,
Or pick my scanty dinner where
All the ground is brown and bare!

The Boy and the Sheep

'Then the farmer comes at last,
When the merry spring is past,
Cuts my woolly fleece away,
For your coat in wintry day;
Little master, that is why
In the pleasant fields I lie.'

Ann Taylor

THE WOODMOUSE

I SAW a little wood-mouse once,
Like Oberon in his hall,
With the green, green moss beneath his feet
Sit under a mushroom tall.

I saw him sit and his dinner eat,
All under the forest tree;
His dinner of the chestnut ripe and red,
And he ate it heartily.

I wish you could have seen him there!
It did my spirit good,
To see the small thing God had made
Thus eating in the wood.

Mary Howitt

CATERPILLAR

Brown and furry
Caterpillar in a hurry,
Take your walk
To the shady leaf, or stalk,
Or what not,
Which may be the chosen spot.
No toad spy you,
Hovering bird of prey pass by you;
Spin and die,
To live again a butterfly.

Christina Rossetti

When JENNY WREN *was* YOUNG

'TWAS on a merry time,
　　When Jenny Wren was young,
So neatly as she danced,
And so sweetly as she sung,
Robin Redbreast lost his heart,
He was a gallant bird,
He doffed his cap to Jenny Wren,
Requesting to be heard.

'My dearest Jenny Wren,
If you will but be mine,
You shall dine on cherry pie
And drink nice currant wine;
I'll dress you like a goldfinch,
Or like a peacock gay,
So if you'll have me, Jenny,
Let us appoint the day.'

When Jenny Wren was Young

Jenny blushed behind her fan
And thus declared her mind—
'So let it be to-morrow Rob,
I'll take your offer kind;
Cherry pie is very good,
And so is currant wine;
But I will wear my plain brown gown
And never dress too fine.'

Robin got up early,
All at the break of day,
He flew to Jenny Wren's house
And sang a roundelay.
A roundelay of love
To pretty Jenny Wren,
And when he came unto the end,
He then began again.

PATHWAYS EVERYWHERE

DUST

I DO not like in summer heat
To walk along the city street:
For dust blows all about my face
And makes my hair its hiding-place.

And when at night I go to bed,
I see quite near me overhead
A golden dust of stars go by
Along the footpaths of the sky.

And in the daytime, if I look
Across the meadows to the brook,
I see, by pathways everywhere,
A silver dust of daisies there.

M. Isabel Foster

THE TIDE

SOMETIMES we peep beneath the blinds,
And through the window bars
We see the dew like silver clouds;
We see the lighted stars;

And down among the sea-weed pools
Where little fishes hide,
Swift coming through the dark we hear
The footsteps of the tide.

We know, when night is tucked away,
To-morrow there will be
Across the flat and shining sand,
The footprints of the sea.

Marjorie Wilson

I'VE BEEN ROAMING

I'VE been roaming, I've been roaming,
Where the meadow-dew is sweet,
And like a queen I'm coming
With its pearls upon my feet.

I've been roaming, I've been roaming,
O'er red rose and lily fair,
And like a sylph I'm coming
With its blossoms in my hair.

I've been roaming, I've been roaming,
Where the honeysuckle creeps,
And like a bee I'm coming
With its kisses on my lips.

I've been roaming, I've been roaming,
Over hill and over plain,
And like a bird I'm coming
To my bower back again.

George Darley

IF ONLY...

If only I'd some money,
 I'd buy a jolly boat
And get a pair of sea-boots
 And a furry sort of coat,
A case or two of salted beef
 And a seaman's wooden chest,
And I'd sail away to the North Pole,
Or I'd sail away to the South Pole,
 Whichever I thought was best.

I'd get up very early—
 They wouldn't see me go—
Jimmy would be with me
 But no one else would know.
Dogs are very useful,
 And I couldn't part with Jim;
But whether I went to the North Pole,
Or whether I went to the South Pole,
 It wouldn't matter to him.

If only . . .

Perhaps we'd see a mountain
    That no one else had seen;
Perhaps we'd find a country
    Where no one else had been
Perhaps we'd climb an iceberg
    And see the midnight sun . . .
Oh, whether we went to the North Pole,
Or whether we went to the South Pole,
    Wouldn't it all be fun!

Rose Fyleman

FROM A RAILWAY CARRIAGE

FASTER than fairies, faster than witches,
Bridges and houses, hedges and ditches,
And charging along like troops in a battle,
All through the meadows the horses and
    cattle:
All of the sights of the hill and the plain
Fly as thick as driving rain;
And ever again, in the wink of an eye,
Painted stations whistle by.

Here is a child who clambers and scrambles,
All by himself and gathering brambles;
Here is a tramp who stands and gazes;
And there is the green for stringing the
    daisies!
Here is a cart run away in the road,
Lumping along with man and load;
And here is a mill, and there is a river;
Each a glimpse and gone for ever!

                        R. L. Stevenson

THE LOST DOLL

I ONCE had a sweet little doll, dears,
    The prettiest doll in the world;
Her cheeks were so red and so white, dears,
    And her hair was so charmingly curled.
But I lost my poor little doll, dears,
    As I played on the heath one day;
And I cried for her more than a week, dears,
    But I never could find where she lay.

I found my poor little doll, dears,
    As I played on the heath one day;
Folks say she is terribly changed, dears,
    For her paint is all washed away,
And her arms trodden off by the cows, dears,
    And her hair not the least bit curled;
Yet for old sake's sake, she is still, dears,
    The prettiest doll in the world.

                      Charles Kingsley

ABOUT BIRDS-NESTING

THE robin and the red-breast,
  The robin and the wren;
If ye take out o' their nest,
Ye'll never thrive agen!

The robin and the red-breast,
The martin and the swallow;
If ye touch one o' their eggs,
Bad luck will surely follow!

(Old Rhyme)

WEATHER WISDOM

Morning and evening

EVENING red and morning grey
Sends the traveller on his way.
But evening grey and morning red
Will bring down rain upon his head.

St Swithin (July 15)

ST Swithin's Day, if thou dost rain,
For forty days it will remain;
St Swithin's Day, if thou be fair,
For forty days 'twill rain nae mair.

The four winds

THE South wind brings wet weather,
The North wind wet and cold together;
The West wind always brings us rain,
The East wind blows it back again.

SECRETS

OH, black blackbird with the shining yellow beak,
You'd tell me why it's yellow, if only you could speak;
I'll tell you why it's yellow, though I can only sing:
I dipped it in a crocus on the first day of Spring.

Oh, blue bluebell on the first summer day,
You'd tell me why your bell's blue, if only you could say;
I'll tell you why my bell's blue, though I can only ring:
A dragon-fly has brushed it with his bright new wing.

Luisa Hewitt

MY LADY

ACROSS the grass, through daisy-snow,
I saw a tripping lady go.

In a gown of bronze with a patterned cloak
She bustled among the sparrow folk.

Hers seemed a very busy life.
She was the Golden Pheasant's wife.

Joan Coster

IN MAY

IN May I go a-walking to hear the linnet sing,
The blackbird and the throstle, a-praising God the King;
It cheers the heart to hear them, to see the leaves unfold,
And the meadows scattered over with buttercups of gold.

SONG IN SPRING

THE silver birch is a dainty lady,
    She wears a satin gown;
The elm-tree makes the old churchyard
    shady,
She will not live in town.

The English oak is a sturdy fellow,
He gets his green coat late;
The willow is smart in a suit of yellow,
While brown the beech-trees wait.

Such a gay green gown God gave the
    larches—
As green as He is good;
The hazels hold up their arms for arches
When Spring rides through the wood.

The chestnut's proud, and the lilac's pretty,
The poplar's gentle and tall,
But the plane-tree's kind to the poor dull
    city—
I love him best of all.

                            E. Nesbit

CITY MOUSE *and* GARDEN MOUSE

THE city mouse lives in a house;—
 The garden mouse lives in a bower,
He's friendly with the frogs and toads,
And sees the pretty plants in flower.

The city mouse eats bread and cheese;—
The garden mouse eats what he can;
We will not grudge him seeds and stalks,
Poor little timid furry man.

Christina Rossetti

MOUSIKIE

THERE was a wee bit mousikie,
    That lived in Gilberaty, O,
It couldna get a bite o'cheese,
    For cheetie-pussie-cattie, O.

It said unto the cheesikie,
    'Oh, fain would I be at ye, O,
If it were na for the cruel paws
    O' cheetie-pussie-cattie, O.'

MARIA'S PURSE

MARIA had an aunt at Leeds,
For whom she made a purse of beads;
'Twas neatly done, by all allow'd,
And praise soon made her vain and proud.

Her mother, willing to repress
This strong conceit of cleverness,
Said, 'I will show you if you please,
A honeycomb, the work of bees!

'Yes, look within their hive, and then
Examine well your purse again;
Compare your merits, and you will
Admit the insects' greater skill!'

                      Elizabeth Turner

OF MYSELF AND MY BATH

IF instead of socks and vest
In fur and feathers I were drest,
Or scales instead of wool and silk,
I'd keep myself as clean as milk.
For Tabby's small pink tongue will do
For soap and sponge and towel too;
And sparrows when they want a bath
Just wallow in the powdered path;
And fishes do not stay a minute
Out of their bath—they're always in it.

Wilfrid Thorley

LOVE BETWEEN BROTHERS AND SISTERS

WHATEVER brawls disturb the street,
    There should be peace at home;
Where sisters dwell and brothers meet,
    Quarrels should never come.

Birds in their little nests agree;
    And 'tis a shameful sight,
When children of one family
    Fall out and chide and fight.

Isaac Watts

A CHILD'S GRACE

SOME hae meat and canna eat,
And some wad eat that want it;
But we hae meat and we can eat,
And sae the Lord be thankit.

      Robert Burns

GOOD NIGHT

LITTLE baby, lay your head
On your pretty cradle-bed;
Shut your eye-peeps, now the day
And the light are gone away;
All the clothes are tucked in tight;
Little baby dear, good-night.

Yes, my darling, well I know
How the bitter wind doth blow;
And the winter's snow and rain
Patter on the window-pane;
But they cannot come in here,
To my little baby dear;

For the window shutteth fast,
Till the stormy night is past;
And the curtains warm are spread
Round about her cradle-bed;
So till morning shineth bright,
Little baby dear, good night.

Jane Taylor

HUSH-A-BA, BIRDIE

HUSH-a-ba, birdie, croon, croon,
Hush-a-ba, birdie, croon.
The sheep are gone to the silver wood
    And the cows are gone to the broom,
       the broom.

And it's braw milking the kye, the kye,
    It's braw milking the kye,
The birds are singing, the bells are ringing,
    And the wild deer come galloping by, by.

And hush-a-ba, birdie, croon, croon,
    Hush-a-by birdie, croon.
The goats are gone to the mountain high,
    And they'll no be hame till noon, noon.

WELL I NEVER

EVERY ONE

IF all the lads beneath the sun—what,
    every one?
Yes, every one,—
Set out for to be sailormen and hied them all
    to sea, O!
Their ships with snowy sails unfurled
Would bridge the width of all the world,
A bridge across dividing seas their dancing
    ships would be, O!

If all the folk beneath the sun—what, every
    one?
Yes, every one—
Would make a ring around the world,
    a wondrous sight to see, O!
If East and West they sallied forth,
From East and West, from South and North,
All hand in hand, round sea and land,
    a goodly ring 'twould be, O!

        A. Thatcher
    (Adapted from the French of Paul Fort)

GOSSIP

'TRAINS are all the fashion,'
　　Said the fairy in the tree,
'They'll catch upon the brambles
When we go for moonlight rambles
And *then* where shall we be?'

'At the caterpillar's wedding,'
Said the Pixie in the moss,
'The dewdrops were so fizzy
That all the guests turned dizzy—
The Queen was very cross.'

'The Weather Clerk's gone crazy,'
Said the Brownie in the fern,
'And all the kinds of weather
Have got mixed up together;
They don't know where to turn.'

'It's nothing else but temper'
Said the Nixie in the pool,
'They've hung him on the spire
With a little bit of wire,
And left him there to cool.'

Gossip

'But have you heard the latest?'
Said the Goblin in the ditch;
'Young Puck has changed the dresses
Of the little twin Princesses,
And they don't know which is which.'

                    Rose Fyleman

THE FOUR PRESENTS

I HAD four brothers over the sea,
Perrie, Merrie, Dixi, Domine;
And they each sent a present unto me.
Petrum, Partrum, Paradisi, Tempore,
Perrie, Merrie, Dixi, Domine.

The first sent a goose without a bone,
Perrie, Merrie, Dixi, Domine;
The second sent a cherry without a stone,
Petrum, Partrum, Paradisi, Tempore,
Perrie, Merrie, Dixi, Domine.

The third sent a blanket without a thread,
Perrie, Merrie, Dixi, Domine;
The fourth sent a book that no man could
    read,
Petrum, Partrum, Paradisi, Tempore,
Perrie, Merrie, Dixi, Domine.

The Four Presents

When the cherry's in the blossom, there is no stone,
Perrie, Merrie, Dixi, Domine;
When the goose is in the egg-shell, there is no bone,
Petrum, Partrum, Paradisi, Tempore,
Perrie, Merrie, Dixi, Domine.

When the wool's on the sheep's back, there is no thread,
Perrie, Merrie, Dixi, Domine;
When the book's in the press, no man can read,
Petrum, Partrum, Paradisi, Tempore,
Perrie, Merrie, Dixi, Domine.

A SPANISH RHYME

TWO little mice went tripping down
 the street,
Pum catta-pum chin chin,
One wore a bonnet and a green silk skirt,
One wore trousers and a nice clean shirt;
Pum catta-pum chin chin.

One little hen went tripping down the street,
Pum catta-pum chin chin,
One little hen very smart and spry,
With a wig-wagging tail and a wicked little
 eye,
Pum catta-pum chin chin.

(Translated by Rose Fyleman)

THE LOBSTER QUADRILLE

'Will you walk a little faster?'
   said the whiting to the snail,
'There's a porpoise close behind me,
   and he's treading on my tail.
See how eagerly the lobsters
   and the turtles all advance!
They are waiting on the shingle—
   will you come and join the dance?
Will you, won't you, will you, won't you,
   won't you join the dance?'

'You can really have no notion
   how delightful it will be
When they take us up and throw us,
   with the lobsters, out to sea!'
But the snail replied, 'Too far, too far!'
   and gave a look askance—

The Lobster Quadrille

Said he thanked the whiting kindly,
 but he would not join the dance.
Would not, could not, would not, could not,
 would not join the dance.

'What matters it how far we go?'
 his scaly friend replied,
'There is another shore, you know,
 upon the other side.
The further off from England
 the nearer is to France—
Then turn not pale, beloved snail,
 but come and join the dance.
Will you, won't you, will you, won't you,
 will you join the dance?
Will you, won't you, will you, won't you,
 won't you join the dance?'

                        Lewis Carroll

THE THREE WELSHMEN

THERE were three jovial Welshmen,
  As I have heard them say,
And they would go a-hunting
Upon St David's day.

All the day they hunted,
And nothing could they find
But a ship a-sailing,
A-sailing with the wind.

One said it was a ship;
The other he said nay;
The third said it was a house,
With the chimney blown away.

The Three Welshmen

And all the night they hunted,
And nothing could they find
But the moon a-gliding,
A-gliding with the wind.

One said it was the moon;
The other he said nay;
The third said it was cheese,
And half o't cut away.

And all the day they hunted,
And nothing could they find
But a hedgehog in a bramble-bush,
And that they left behind.

The first said it was a hedgehog,
The second he said nay;
The third it was a pin-cushion,
And the pins stuck the wrong way.

The Three Welshmen

And all the night they hunted,
And nothing could they find
But a hare in a turnip field,
And that they left behind.

The first said it was a hare;
The second he said nay;
The third said it was a calf,
And the cow had run away.

And all the day they hunted,
And nothing could they find
But an owl in a holly-tree,
And that they left behind.

One said it was an owl;
The other he said nay;
The third said 'twas an old man,
And his beard growing grey.

TOM THIMBLE

TOM Thimble lives
 In the whitethorn tree.
  Many pale flowers
Nod round his knee,
  Nod round his head
Where goldilocks be.
  Tom Thimble lives
In the whitethorn tree.

  Tom Thimble dines
In the whitethorn tree.
  Eats honey-wafers
Brought by a bee,
  Drinks deep o' dew
Out o' blossoms wee.
  Tom Thimble dines
In the whitethorn tree.

Tom Thimble

Tom Thimble's wife
In the whitethorn tree,
   Sews a little coat
Made of rosemarie.
   All its little seams
Smell sweet as sweet can be,
   Stitched among the scents
Of the whitethorn tree.

   Tom Thimble's child
In the whitethorn tree,
   Is much too small
For anyone to see.
   There they peep and peer,
A teeny-weeny three—
   Tom Thimble and his wife and child,
In the whitethorn tree.

                          Blanche Winder

JONATHAN
(A Dutch rhyme)

JONATHAN Gee
Went out with his cow;
He climbed up a tree
And sat on a bough.
He sat on a bough
And it broke in half,
And John's old cow
Did nothing but laugh.
(Translated by Rose Fyleman.)

THE LOST SHOE

POOR little Lucy
  By some mischance,
Lost her shoe
  As she did dance:
'Twas not on the stairs,
  Not in the hall;
Not where they sat
  At supper at all.
She looked in the garden,
  But there it was not;
Henhouse, or kennel,
  Or high dove cote.
Dairy and meadow
  And wild woods through
Showed not a trace
  Of Lucy's shoe.
Bird nor bunny
  Nor glimmering moon

The Lost Shoe

Breathed a whisper
   Of where 'twas gone.
It was cried and cried,
   Oyez and Oyez!
In French, Dutch, Latin,
   And Portuguese.
Ships the dark seas
   Went plunging through,
But none brought news
   Of Lucy's shoe;
And still she patters
   In silk and leather,
O'er snow and shingle,
   In every weather;
Spain, and Africa,
   Hindustan,
Java, China,
   And lamped Japan;

The Lost Shoe

Plain and desert,
   She hops—hops through,
Pernambuco
   To gold Peru;
Mountain and forest,
   And river too,
All the world over
   For her lost shoe.

Walter de la Mare

A SONG FOR HAL

ONCE I saw a little boat,
and a pretty, pretty boat,
   When daybreak the hills was adorning,
And into it I jumped,
and away I did float,
   So very, very, early in the morning.

CHORUS
For every little wave has its nightcap on,
Its nightcap, white cap, nightcap on,
For every little wave has its nightcap on,
So very, very early in the morning.

A Song for Hal

All the fishes were asleep
in their caves cool and deep,
When the ripple round my keel flashed a
 warning;
Said the minnow to the skate,
'We must certainly be late,
Though I thought 'twas very early in the
 morning.'

CHORUS
For every little wave has its nightcap on,
Its nightcap, white cap, nightcap on,
For every little wave has its nightcap on,
So very, very early in the morning.

The lobster, darkly green,
soon appeared upon the scene,
And pearly drops his claws were adorning;
Quoth he, 'May I be boiled,
if I'll have my pleasure spoiled
So very, very early in the morning.'

A Song for *Hal*

CHORUS
For every little wave has its nightcap on,
Its nightcap, white cap, nightcap on,
For every little wave has its nightcap on,
So very, very early in the morning.

Said the sturgeon to the eel,
'Just imagine how I feel
Thus roused without a syllable of warning;
People ought to let us know
when a-sailing they would go
So very, very early in the morning.'

CHORUS
When every little wave has its nightcap on,
Its nightcap, white cap, nightcap on,
When every little wave has its nightcap on,
So very, very early in the morning.

Just then, up jumped the sun,
and the fishes every one

A Song for Hal

For their laziness at once fell a-mourning.
But I stayed to hear no more,
for my boat had reached the shore,
So very, very early in the morning.

CHORUS
*For every little wave has its nightcap on,
Its nightcap, white cap, nightcap on,
For every little wave has its nightcap on,
So very, very early in the morning.*

And every little wave took its nightcap off,
Its nightcap, white cap, nightcap off,
And every little wave took its nightcap off,
And curtsied to the sun in the morning.

Laura Richards

THE FROG AND THE CROW

A JOLLY fat frog lived in the river
    swim, O!
A comely black crow lived on the river
    brim, O!
'Come on shore, come on shore,' said the
    crow to the frog, and then, O!
'No, you'll bite me, no, you'll bite me,'
    Said the frog to the crow again, O!

'O! there is sweet music on yonder green
    hill, O!
And you shall be a dancer, a dancer all in
    yellow,
All in yellow, all in yellow,'
Said the crow to the frog, and then, O!
'All in yellow, all in yellow,'
Said the frog to the crow again, O!

The Frog and the Crow

'Farewell, ye little fishes, that in the river swim, O!
I'm going to be a dancer, a dancer in yellow.'
'O beware! O beware!'
Said the fish to the frog, and then, O!
'I'll take care, I'll take care,'
Said the frog to the fish again, O!

The frog began a-swimming, a-swimming to land, O!
And the crow began jumping to give him his hand, O!
'Sir, you're welcome, Sir, you're welcome,'
Said the crow to the frog, and then, O!
'Sir, I thank you, Sir, I thank you,'
Said the frog to the crow again, O!

The Frog and the Crow

'But where is the sweet music on yonder green
    hill, O?
And where are all the dancers, the dancers in
    yellow?
All in yellow, all in yellow?'
Said the frog to the crow, and then, O!
'Sir, they're here, Sir, they're here.'
Said the crow to the frog—

      (Here the crow swallows the frog)

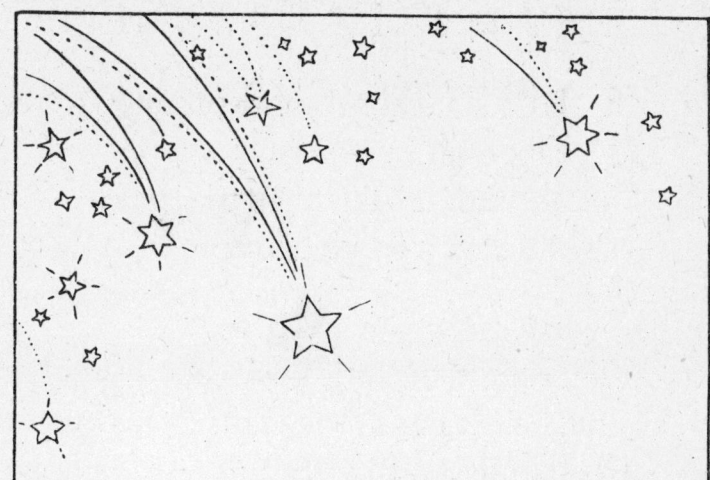

DREAMS & STARSHINE

THE LITTLE DREAMER

A LITTLE boy was dreaming
Upon his nurse's lap
That the pins fell out of all the stars,
And the stars fell into his cap.

So when the dream was over,
What should the little boy do?
Why, he went and looked inside his cap,
And found it wasn't true.

      D' A. W. Thompson

LIGHT THE LAMPS UP LAMPLIGHTER

For a Lamplighter, a Grandmother, The Angel Gabriel, and Any Number of others.

LIGHT the lamps up, Lamplighter,
The people are in the street—
　　Without a light
　　They have no sight,
And where will they plant their feet?

Some will tread in the gutter,
And some in the mud—oh dear!
Light the lamps up, Lamplighter,
Because the night is here.

Light the Lamps

Light the candles, Grandmother,
The children are going to bed—
      Without a wick
         They'll stumble and stick,
And where will they lay their head?

Some will lie on the staircase,
And some in the hearth—oh dear!
Light the candles, Grandmother,
Because the night is here.

Light the stars up, Gabriel,
The cherubs are out to fly—
      If heaven is blind
         How will they find
Their way across the sky?

Light the Lamps

Some will splash in the Milky Way,
Or bump on the moon—oh, dear!
Light the stars up, Gabriel,
Because the night is here.

Eleanor Farjeon

KINGS CAME RIDING

KINGS came riding,
One, two and three,
Over the desert
And over the sea.

One in a ship
With a silver mast;
The fishermen wondered
As he went past.

One on a horse
With a saddle of gold;
The children came running
To behold.

One came walking,
Over the sand,
With a casket of treasure
Held in his hand.

Kings came Riding

All the people
Said 'Where go they?'
But the kings went forward
All through the day.

Night came on
As those kings went by;
They shone like the gleaming
Stars in the sky.

                Charles Williams

CRADLE HYMN

WITH straw for his pillow, a manger his bed,
Little Lord Jesus laid down his dear head;
The stars in the heavens looked down where he lay,
Little Lord Jesus asleep in the hay.

The cattle are lowing, the baby awakes,
But little Lord Jesus, no crying he makes.
I love thee, Lord Jesus, look down from the sky,
And stay by my bed until morning is nigh.

(Translated from Martin Luther)

OLD CAROL

GOD bless the master of this house,
The mistress also,
    And all the little childeren
        That round the table go.
    And all your kin and kinsmen,
        That dwell both far and near,
I wish you a merry Christmas
        And a happy New Year.

NOV 1960